"A wonderful, compelling story of human com

—Mike Balla, MSW, RSW, Balla Consulting Group, Inc.

"Airdrie Thompson-Guppy is a pioneer. ... We learn about the early days of a system of foster care before it was a system; we learn a lot about expectations, both realistic and unrealistic; and, last but not least, we learn that lives can be enhanced (even if not entirely transformed) by the care of strangers."

—Robert Glossop, CM, PhD, Hon. DSc, Hon. LLD;
former Executive Director of Programs for
the Vanier Institute of the Family

"*Airdrie's Boys* is a candid and insightful personal reflection on life's journeys. ... Her story will be an echo for all of us who care about, and have cared for, special children. It will remind us of the foundational impact on our personal and professional lives made by the young people we encountered in our fledgling careers, who worried us, gave us hope, taught us and made us ask the kind of questions that Airdrie Thompson-Guppy still asks."

—Ron Ensom, MSW, RSW, author of
If Your Child Is Abused

"The voices of the boys, their troubles, struggles, successes, in true-to-life stories, are both heartwrenching and heartwarming. The genuineness of the life paths described will speak to foster parents, foster children, anyone considering fostering and anyone who cares about children."

—Dr. Dennis Kimberley, Professor of Social Work,
Memorial University, Newfoundland, Canada

Airdrie's boys were very fortunate that their attachment to Airdie was not determined by the length of the CAS project. Her book will give a new light to the ideal role of foster parents, particularly where seriously traumatized, delinquent adolescents are concerned. Or is she a life long attachment fi gure they never had?

—Dr. Kati Morrison, Psychiatrist, co-author of *Stepmothers: Exploring the Myth. A Survival Guide for Stepfamilies*

Airdrie's personal recollections are interesting, insightful, and informative but more importantly are instructive as they help us appreciate the fundamental importance of relationships. She highlights for us the reality that, when working with vulnerable young people, we sometimes just don't know exactly what works, what doesn't work and why.

—Dan Wiseman, BSW, MSW
Ottawa, Ontario

AIRDRIE'S BOYS

Fostering as a Family Form

A story that began by chance
and ended as a gift.

AIRDRIE THOMPSON-GUPPY

iUniverse, Inc.
Bloomington

Airdrie's Boys
Fostering as a Family Form

iUniverse books may be ordered through booksellers or by contacting:

iUniverse
1663 Liberty Drive
Bloomington, IN 47403
www.iuniverse.com
1-800-Authors (1-800-288-4677)

ISBN: 978-1-4759-3048-1 (sc)
ISBN: 978-1-4759-3050-4 (hc)
ISBN: 978-1-4759-3049-8 (e)

Printed in the United States of America

iUniverse rev. date: 07/10/2012

For Diane—
who inspired me in writing my stories, and whom the world
suddenly and sadly lost on
November 24, 2000

One must wait until the evening
to see how splendid the day has been.

—Socrates

FOREWORD

In her book *Airdrie's Boys*, Airdrie provides us a remarkable story of how she, as a nurturing foster parent, formed lasting lifetime connections with a group of boys in child welfare care even though the boys were in her care for a relatively short period of time. It is an example of the power of one person, who brings unconditional acceptance and nurturance to a child, to provide a pathway to encouragement and hope as a replacement for discouragement and despair. The attachment that was formed with these boys, and the sense of belonging and safety that it provided, offered hope, stability and a set positive of values and expectations that were a frame of reference that influenced the boys throughout adulthood.

Research into the world of newborns has shown that we are social by nature. The newest publications on brain research point to the brain being wired for social connections. Scientists refer to "the social brain" and highlight the need for attachments to stimulate the brain for healthy adaptive responses to everyday life. The need for attachment and belonging continues throughout our lifetimes.

We require connections to a social group to develop a sense of well-being. Children require a safe and secure environment with strong emotional and physical attachments to one or more significant adults to develop successfully. A child's need to belong is paramount to a healthy foundation on which to build all future relationships. Airdrie shows us the power of the foster parent to meet the developmental needs of children and their fundamental need to be important to someone, to know that someone cares deeply about them.

Having known Airdrie for more than 40 years as colleague and friend, I have seen her as a woman who makes a difference in any relationship she enters. She models acceptance, security and safety with clear expectations and boundaries for family living. This was reflected in her relationship with the boys. She was clear that these boys already had families and encouraged ongoing connections which respected their family history, past and present—relationships that are intended to last a lifetime.

As foster families, we become part of the "village that raises children." Airdrie was willing to risk trying new models of care, new mental health strategies and investment in the future of children and youth. She was a trailblazer and a role model in working with the unknown and learning from her foster youth.

This book is filled with examples of tenacity, resilience and trust that build as families face the challenges of life together. Airdrie represented a beacon in the life storms that these boys, now men, managed. She offered them guidance, respect and a common bond with each other having lived in the same foster family.

As is so evident in this story, we often do not appreciate the long-term impact of investing in a child's life until much later when we come to witness the growth that has occurred from the seeds that were planted years earlier.

This book is a testimony to foster care in all its forms and clearly demonstrates the adage, "It takes a village to raise a child." Foster parents are heroes in our communities and deserve to have their stories recorded as they create families for children who require alternate care and they substantially increase a child's life chances.

Through her book, Airdrie honours her boys and applauds the importance of safe and loving havens that foster families provide for children and youth who deserve to grow up in healthy and supportive environments.

Marion Balla
President
Adlerian Counselling and Consulting Group

CONTENTS

PREFACE

A family provides a child with the basic parameters for functioning in society later in life. Family can take many forms, and the family form has been a subject that has always interested me. My first book was about stepfamilies, which now can be found in most extended family circles. Although stepfamilies have greater visibility and often more success than they did 25 years ago, the issues that they face remain the same. And because there are more stepfamilies today, an individual family's "constellation" is generally far more complex than it once might have been.

As a result, a child may be part of two very different kinds of families—with two dads or two moms on one side, for example, and a dad and a mom on the other side. Very often, a child's biological parents will live in separate cities or even separate countries. Sometimes only one parent remains in the child's life, while the other fades away. And then there are the problems that come with differences of religion and culture within a family—problems that might be ignored until they surface when the children grow older. Today young children cross cultural boundaries with initial ease, but as they grow older, they very often face clashing expectations from different sides of their family. Of course, miscommunication and poorly defined parenting roles are at the base of some of these misunderstandings; if the root issues are not addressed, the problems become increasingly complicated.

For these daunting reasons, I decided to write about one family form that I have experienced in my own life. In fact, until I wrote my little story, I had not considered fostering children to be a family form. At first, I saw my role as more of a job: rescuing or protecting children and adolescents who were in a lot of trouble and whose families were dysfunctional and unable to cope with their child's behaviour. But having lived through an experimental year to see if running a group home was a viable option for me, and having had the extraordinary opportunity to have ongoing contact with some of the boys, I now have a very different view of fostering.

What I learned from my experience is that understanding the history and sometimes hidden pain that children bring to their new home situation might alter adults' approach to their care and treatment. This is true not just for foster families, but also for stepfamilies and many other family forms as well.

At the time of my involvement, a group home was considered an extension of foster care. (Today, the two are viewed differently, with group homes often cast in a far more negative light.) My boys were with us in an effort to keep them out of adult institutions. At the time, it did not occur to me that I was putting my family at risk by inviting them into our home—and that naïveté may have been the reason they integrated in a successful manner. They did indeed face serious consequences later in life, but they never forgot the brief interlude of acceptance in our home. Even when the fostering period is relatively brief, if the experience is positive and the child feels accepted and included, the resulting boost to his self-esteem can carry him a long way in life.

Another factor in the success of my fostering experience was the tremendous support and recognition that I received over the year. I was able to consult with professional staff and a psychiatrist at a regular monthly meeting—not a typical benefit for foster parents. And many neighbours and acquaintances lent their support as well. At Christmas, for example, my husband's secretary gave us a turkey for the boys to enjoy.

It was also my natural instinct to be receptive to those biological parents who wondered who I was and who continued to show concern for their children. It was important for them to see that I did not consider their boys an imposition; caring for someone else's children needs to be a normal part of family life, and not just a job.

After the fostering period ended, I never invited the boys back to have an ongoing relationship with us, but they did come by from time to time for a visit or to bring news of their own activities; each boy defined those boundaries in his own way. Later in their lives, they would identify particular incidents with our family that left a positive, permanent mark on them. Whether they stayed with us for two weeks or nine months, the boys were part of a functioning family.

Temporary as it might be, I think we need to study foster care in a new light so that, at the very least, foster children get a message that this is a family that welcomes them and cares about them, and that there is a place for them within the family structure. I believe that foster care has generally been seen simply as temporary placement while a child's long-term care is being planned out. Even if the foster home is a very nurturing one, it is generally not considered a family form that can be a real investment in the life of a child. Granted, the child might not respond immediately, but at least he is given that initial chance to feel accepted and cared for. All children—biological or adopted children, stepchildren or foster children—need to hear a strong message that they are individuals, that their own history and perceptions are important and that they have a place where they belong.

From October 1963 to December 1964, my husband and I fostered five boys in a group home for the Children's Aid Society for the County of Waterloo in Ontario. The boys were with us for varying lengths of time, and we usually had only two boys at once. The society had not sponsored a group home before, so we were given few guidelines, but we agreed to be part of the program for one year. In hindsight, I recognize that this was not a long enough period of time to demonstrate the effectiveness of group fostering. Nevertheless, it was a positive, life-changing experience for us and for five adolescent boys who were in a great deal of trouble. The Children's Aid Society seemed equally pleased, as indicated in the board minutes included at the end of this story and by the fact that the CAS went on to create two more group homes the following year.

Last year, 47 years after they lived in our home, three of the boys came to visit me. We were all very different people, of course, and it was wonderful to discover the adults they had become.

Lefty saw me as a woman rather than as a mom. He loves cars, so he was quite surprised and pleased when I drove them to our local hockey arena and then to sightsee around the city without any problem. He thought I did pretty well! I saw him as a happy 60-year-old man who had delved into criminal behaviour but fortunately had grown out of it and surfaced to pick up his life and mend the broken parts—quite successfully, I might add.

Dan was a 59-year-old who was both grown up and as cheery and interesting as he was as a boy. He had developed some insight into what society expected of him, and he had learned to communicate very effectively.

Bob joined us but only half-heartedly, as he had not conquered his life problems. Still, he did not want to miss anything.

They told me stories I had never heard before about our time as a family, and they said there were some stories that they still could not tell me. I, in turn, reminded them of some of their mischievous and worrisome behaviour—which, interestingly, they did not remember. In that respect, our reunion was a scenario any family would recognize.

Over the course of our discussions, we all decided that it would be worthwhile for me to write their story. When I explained that it would be important to change their names for the sake of confidentiality, each man put forth a new name without blinking an eye. When I mentioned the plan to my daughter, who is mentioned primarily at the beginning of the story, she decided that she, too, would take on a new name. Hence, we have Trisha! My second husband was and is Jack, because that is how everyone knew and loved him.

This is a story for anyone who cares about children. It is for families, to give them confidence that lives can change and mend. It is for all the social workers, psychologists, ministers, child care specialists and therapists, lawyers and judges who make the decisions that impact children. I was not a part of those decisions for my boys, and I believe my voice should have been heard. While it's true that they indeed broke the law or their behaviour was unmanageable in their own homes, their actions should not have been the only important considerations in their treatment. Their life histories were important too—as was mine. As the sister of adopted siblings, I had experienced yet another family form, which probably helped me have a naturally accepting approach to my foster children.

This is a story from me, Airdrie, and from "my boys."

CHAPTER 1

THE GROUP HOME

1963–64

In 1963 my first husband, Evan, and I moved to Waterloo, Ontario, with our one-year-old daughter, Trisha. We had just come through a very traumatic year, but Waterloo seemed to be a delightful little city, and we settled in nicely. My days were tedious—I spent most of them alone with Trisha, as Evan worked very long hours. We were in an apartment building in a newly developed area on the edge of town, but because everyone was new, it was fun meeting and talking to our neighbours. I remember watching TV with disbelief when President John Kennedy was assassinated; although they were troubling times, we seemed safe and far removed from it all in Waterloo.

When I agreed to provide day care to three other children in our building, my days became busier and full of fun. I felt as if I were running my own little school. We had outdoor play, when I would walk the children across the street to see the cows in the fields. Indoor play was crayoning and whatever else four children under the age of three could manage. There was TV time, rest time, snack time—we did it all. But 15 dollars per extra child per week (one was already mine) did not work out to much additional income. So at the end of the year, when two of the children moved away, I decided I had to get a job outside the home.

Because I had been a social worker in both Montreal and Toronto, I felt I would have no difficulty getting a job. In Montreal I had worked with foster families, helping them deal with the many challenges that confronted them. I was 21 at the time, and I wonder now how those foster mothers really felt about my visits. But they seemed to like me, and I was by nature very supportive of their efforts, having come from a nontraditional family. I was the eldest of five children—the three youngest a set of triplets who were adopted at the age of 22 months. So I already understood something about integrating children into an established family and recognizing their normal but special needs, and I knew the hard work that was involved.

In 1961 I worked in what was then called the "Unwed Mothers Department" in Toronto. I loved my job counselling the young women, discussing their circumstances and helping them sort out what they wanted to do. Most were on their own; many had not even confided in their families. Out of my caseload of 30 young women, it was considered permissible if one decided to keep her baby. Twice in that year I was sharply chastised by my matronly supervisor—each time because I had two mothers keeping their babies. Really, I mustn't have been doing my work properly, and even worse, I was skewing the statistics! I worked for a few more months and then discreetly resigned.

Three years later, armed with my own beliefs about recognizing clients' needs, I applied to the Waterloo Children's Aid Society. I assumed that like most social agencies, the CAS always needed staff. With a résumé that included a bachelor's degree in psychology, two summers in Montreal working with foster parents and then my year working at the Toronto CAS with unwed mothers, I felt certain the Kitchener-Waterloo CAS would be impressed with my experience.

I arrived at my appointment with the director feeling confident. He scanned my résumé, and then, without commenting on my experience, looked directly at me and remarked that I had a daughter who was nearly two—and I should go home and look after her. I was shocked; it was clear to me that there was to be no further discussion.

Trisha was bright, and she was used to being with other children; surely she would fit into a day care setting. But the thinking of the day, at least in Waterloo, was that young mothers should not work outside the home. That mentality did not fit my cosmopolitan view, but it certainly took the wind out of my sails. It did not occur to me to apply anywhere else.

Looking back now, I realize that the societal norms regarding working moms were still in transition, and the little city of Waterloo was not keeping pace with the Montreal girl who thought that mothers should do whatever was necessary and that they could cover all the bases.

But the CAS kept my résumé and apparently took note of my work history. A month or so after my meeting with the director, I received a call from Mrs. Simon, a CAS staff member. She wanted to visit me to discuss a new project the agency hoped to undertake. I told her that would be fine. I had no idea what the project was about.

Mrs. Simon arrived accompanied by another staff member. Both were very pleasant and interested in my family. They noted my experience, particularly with foster parents, and they proceeded to explain the concept of a group home—like a foster home, but taking more than one child at a time. The group home the CAS envisioned would be for boys between the ages of 13 and 16 who had experienced significant difficulty in their own homes or in the community.

The project was to be funded by monies that had been used to support an orphanage in Kitchener-Waterloo called Willow Hall. Many traditional orphanages were being closed by the province because there were fewer orphans, and those children who did require care were being integrated into foster homes. So funding for the orphanage was made available to CAS to use for ongoing work with children.

It's apparent to me in hindsight that the exact plan was not clear, but the CAS felt it would develop along the way. This new program was to be a resource for adolescent boys who were in significant trouble but who did not belong in an adult institution. The number of boys involved was undetermined; it was possible that some would come through the court system. And although the boys would be required to attend school, there was no plan in place for their daily care or for therapeutic services.

As our discussion unfolded, the younger of the two women tried to explain that the group home would be like a foster home but on a larger scale. Her pretty face darkened as she explained that these would be the most serious cases—the CAS was trying to keep the boys out of training school or jail. The older woman nodded in agreement, and while she looked concerned for me, she also seemed to be acknowledging what I may be able to do; after all, I did have experience working with children. She would turn out to be a strong support for me through all the adventures of that year.

When they asked if I would take on the project, I was shocked by their proposal. Yes, I had a little day care project, but that was with preschoolers. And yes, I had dealt with families, but that was as a social worker, working out of an office. I was a serious professional. I did not take children into my home full-time, particularly when they were half-grown and in a lot of trouble. No, no—I could not do that job. No! And so they left. I did not give it another thought.

But a month later I received another call from Mrs. Simon, asking if we could meet again to follow up. I agreed, and this time the women described how Evan and I could pick out a house that would accommodate our family of three plus four foster children. They would pay the rent, buy our appliances and furnish the bedrooms. They would also, of course, supply the foster children. The plan became more interesting, but I was still overwhelmed.

"No, I don't think so," I said quietly. I did give it some thought, though. And free rent—what a disgraceful point to consider, under these serious circumstances—would really help us! It was a long, hard decision, but finally Evan and I came to the conclusion that we would give it an honest try. Evan had a secure and interesting job, and this new plan would enable me to continue taking care of Trisha at home. The three of us were in good health and spirits, and hopefully we had something to offer. That was in October 1964. I was 24 years old.

I don't think I signed a formal contract, but whatever the terms were, I essentially had carte blanche to do whatever I considered helpful and right in caring for the boys. There was no discussion about any issues or problems the boys might have or how I might (or must not) address them. There was no training for foster parents in those days, and the CAS did not seem to have a model from any other group home in the province. There was no discussion about accountability of any kind, and there was no thought about safety measures on the part of CAS—or on our part, either. Evan and I were given no direction about choosing a location or how our neighbours might react to our presence. It was just a pilot project that would unfold in its own way.

But as we discussed it further, the whole idea became more exciting and challenging to Evan and me. It would be my job, mainly, as he was very busy with his work, but he was supportive and planned to be involved whenever he could be. And in fact, he got to work right away, making two sets of bunk beds for the boys' rooms. We also bought a small bureau for each boy. As a social worker in Montreal, I had seen situations where children had their own beds to sleep in but only an orange crate to hold their belongings.

Jane, one of the CAS representatives, took me shopping one afternoon, and for $475 I was able to pick out a beautiful stove, a large fridge and a matching washer and dryer. Oh my gosh, I was so happy! We moved into a split-level, four-bedroom home, where most of our own furniture fit in nicely. It seemed to be a quiet neighbourhood, and apparently the CAS hadn't told the neighbours anything about us. As a young couple with a darling little girl, we were easily accepted. During the weekdays, the boys were at school most of the time, and on weekends we often went out and did things together.

Over the course of the next year, we would have five boys in our care, staying for various amounts of time and for various reasons.

CHAPTER 2

LEFTY

December 1963–July 1964

We had been in the house for only two weeks when the first boy, Lefty, arrived. All I was told was that he had a problem with his father.

Lefty was 15, the second of four children, and despite his bad home life, he had a friendly, relaxed manner. He was of average height, with straight brown hair brushed to the side. He smoked and had very bad teeth, but you were distracted from that by his sparkling eyes and easy smile.

Lefty's father was in the armed forces, and his family was living in Africa when he was born. His father was away at the time; his mother delivered him on the living room floor, which she had spread with newspaper. Perhaps as a result, Lefty's father didn't bond with him and, in fact, questioned whether Lefty was indeed his child. I believe this strengthened the bond between mother and son, particularly as the years went by.

There was continual conflict—verbal and physical—between Lefty's parents, and because he felt some responsibility and wanted to protect his mother, Lefty often would act out to redirect his father's anger toward himself. As a result, Lefty's father would punish him severely, sometimes in extreme ways. At one stage he chained Lefty to the swing set outside so that everyone could see him. This experience had a profound effect on Lefty, and he was only able to resolve his anger and find some peace years later, when I took him to visit his father's grave. There he had a long talk with his father, who he felt could now understand and accept him.

Because of the ongoing conflict, Lefty's father wanted him out of the house, and so he was taken to the CAS. Viewing him as an out-of-control child, the agency placed him with us. However, he adjusted easily to our family and was particularly taken with our two-year-old daughter, Trisha. He was protective of her and played very carefully with her, saying she was like a little sister to him. Lefty was able to continue going to his same school with his friends. Our home was only a few blocks from that of his parents—a fact that Lefty considered weird—but somehow that proximity was not taken into account at the time of his placement. In fact, his mother came to visit on occasion, and she seemed reassured that he had settled into our home and that we were quite happy to have him. His father, on the other hand, never came by or called. Lefty later told me how guilty he felt at the time, not being at home to protect his mom. On the other hand, his new, peaceful environment gave him some comfort.

There were other interesting challenges with Lefty. Although I was just 24 and he was 15, he decided he would call me Mom because he could not pronounce my name. So when we went to the store to buy clothes—I had a CAS charge card for these excursions—Lefty would go to the opposite end of the store and call out, "Mom!" Of course, people would stare at this young-looking woman with a young child, and then at Lefty, who was so much older. He loved it! Then we would go to the counter to pay. Inevitably, the girl at the checkout would look at my card and then call (it sounded like hollering to me), "I have a CAS card here—I need help!"

Then there was the morning when I stripped the sheets off Lefty's bed and, in doing so, moved the mattress slightly. There, poking out from under the mattress, was some kind of magazine I had never seen before. I pulled it out and … *Oh my God, what is this?* There were photos of scantily clad girls in various poses and doing various activities that I had never even imagined—probably because of my own strict and rigid upbringing. But that did not hinder my curiosity. I set down my cleaning supplies, sat down on the edge of Lefty's bed and about two hours later finally went back to work. Whew! What an education. I made the bed and tucked the magazine under the mattress, where it belonged.

Lefty mixed well with the other boys who came to live with us during his stay. In the summer of 1964, he was nearly 16—the upper limit for CAS care—so it was decided that he would return home. I believe that since there had been no particular incidents of concern, the agency thought it was safe for him to move back. There was little discussion about it, but his mother was very pleased. His father seemed to have a change of heart and offered Lefty a car if he would behave. That was the drawing card, and Lefty departed, happily believing his life would continue as it had been at our home. Unfortunately, there had been no discussion of or preparation for his transition on the family's end. Because his family continued to function as it always had, Lefty quickly slid back into his old role.

By then, Lefty was too old to return to care at CAS, but he left home anyway. He dropped out of school and drifted around, sometimes staying with his friend Ed. He showed up regularly at our place, particularly at suppertime, but he also enjoyed seeing the other boys because they were his old family. On occasion he would even stay overnight, but I could never get him to take a bath!

Eventually Lefty got a job at a local gas station, where he became well respected and quickly learned the trade. He managed to save some money to buy an old car of his own, and that made all the difference in the world to him.

Of course, there was never enough money. So he made friends with those who could help him get more—the wrong more—and soon he was drinking, drugging and selling. Lefty understood that he could not bring this behaviour to our door. When he came to visit, he was sober, and he seemed to want to continue to see the other boys and be the big brother in the family. Continuing these contacts was still important to him. To my knowledge, he did not share his vices with the younger boys.

Around 1967, three years after our group fostering project was finished, Lefty finally went to jail for his activities, and he called me and asked me to visit him. I asked a friend to go with me because I had never been to a jail before, much less visited someone I knew there. It was a bit traumatic for me, but Lefty seemed fine and seemed to consider the experience as just a brief chapter in his life. I tried not to think about it.

In 1968, when Lefty was 20, he met a girl named Sally, and their relationship really redirected him in a positive fashion. They were two lost souls with significant family issues, and they thrived together, bringing out the very best in each other. Life was good—they were both happy and working.

One day Lefty came to me, very excited. He had put some money down on a beautiful little watch on a gold chain. Sally would love it, he said, and he was going to work hard to pay it off before he gave it to her. When that day finally came, he brought the watch over to the house to show me. It was lovely, and I shared his joy. But then I saw that there was not just one watch, but two: one for Sally, and one for me. There are no words, even now, to describe how I felt. *Should I accept it?* There were so many questions whirling around in my head. But of course I did. After all, I was Lefty's mom.

Sally and Lefty were soon married—she was 17, and he was 22. Three years later, they had a baby girl, Summer Airdrie.

Summer was born nine weeks early, weighing only two pounds, six ounces. The smallest diapers were too big for her; the nurses had to use facecloths. Lefty called her Peanut.

Lefty was afraid to celebrate her birth because he did not know whether or not she would live. He talked about how frightened he was to be a parent and how worried he was that he would be a hindrance to her. He did not want her to pick up his bad habits as she grew up. Later he recognized that he was afraid of bonding with the baby in case she did not survive. However, Summer rallied, survived and thrived, and her parents were finally able to take her home.

Now Lefty had real responsibilities. For two years, he and Sally did the best they could to nurture and love their baby girl. They did enjoy some family support, but both sets of parents continued to be preoccupied by their own issues.

They tried, but Lefty knew he could not live up to Sally's aspirations of a white-picket-fence kind of life. He slowly reverted back to doing and dealing drugs, which of course did not enhance their family life. After three years of struggling, they divorced. Sally had a good job and was able to arrange stable day care; Lefty felt certain that she would be all right if he was not around. Sally, on the other hand, had to deal with the many challenges of being a single mother. It was a very difficult time for her. To this day, however, they both maintain that their early relationship and marriage was good for them at that time in their lives.

One weekend, before they separated, Lefty and Sally visited, bringing along Dan, another boy who had stayed in our home; Lefty and Dan had continued to keep in touch. I did not know until years later that Dan always got drunk on Saturday nights—he thought that was what Saturday nights were for. However, he knew that if he came to visit me, he could not get drunk, so he decided to drink on Thursday night instead. It was a pretty rough drive for him with Lefty the next day, but he seemed to enjoy the weekend with us.

Unfortunately, it was not long before Lefty's life became even more complicated.

His lifestyle and financial situation led to depression, and over the years he did not see much of his daughter. He knew that Sally had moved ahead with her life and a new relationship, and he understood at some level that Jason, her new partner, was providing for Summer both financially and emotionally. But when he realized that Sally and Jason and the two children—Summer and a new baby—were visiting me in my home, he became very angry with me. He was content with Sally and Summer continuing their relationship with me, but he could not tolerate the fact that Jason would be there too.

He called to tell me that I had ruined his life and that he would never speak to me again. He ranted and criticized me for several minutes and then slammed down the phone. I was speechless and overwhelmed, but I decided to let it rest for a while.

I did not hear from Lefty again until 20 years later, when Summer was about to graduate from university and he realized he might see me at the ceremony. I am not sure what the exact occasion was—I could not go to the graduation—but we crossed that bridge quite easily and began communicating once again.

I encouraged Lefty to seek therapy closer to home, which he did, happily sharing some of his progress with me. His therapist assured him that he had not necessarily been a bad kid, but that he regularly tried to deflect his father's aggression away from his mother to himself. Then, when his father finally kicked him out, he felt guilty that he could no longer protect his mother.

Through therapy, Lefty began to understand why he'd turned to drugs and alcohol following his time with us and when he was out on his own. He seemed to be afraid to grow up. The pain of his earlier life was always with him. He did manage to settle down during his first years with Sally, but then he became involved with drugs again, which led to the breakup of his marriage. Lefty now tells me he's glad for the experiences he had because they made him the person he is today. Both he and Sally appreciate the years they had together, even though they finally went their separate ways.

Although Lefty was getting professional counselling, he wanted to talk to me about his relationship with Summer. He began calling me on a monthly basis, and our talks seemed to enhance and clarify the counselling process. Between his counselling sessions and our discussions, he began to understand why his relationship with Summer was unsatisfying. He began to recognize that when they visited, he would talk as quickly as he could about all the things he knew about and what he was doing. That left little time for Summer to tell him about herself, and it was not really a meaningful relationship for her.

With a great deal of coaching and encouragement, Lefty learned to ask questions and then listen to what Summer had to say. Indeed, he got to know and cherish his little girl, who had grown up to be a very accomplished businesswoman and a happily married wife. That gave them both a whole new perspective on their relationship and a real reason to look forward to seeing each other—not often, but on special occasions.

Lefty had been away from Canada for many years and had found himself in a number of dangerous situations. He never wanted to discuss these things in any detail. All I know is that he managed to survive, and it is not clear what brought that chapter of his life to a close. However, he did return to Canada, where he was able to pick up some of the pieces of his life and move forward. His good progress enhanced his self-esteem, which in turn broadened his interests and friendships.

Lefty lived in a rent-to-income apartment, and over the years he was very helpful to many of his neighbours, assisting with their banking, grocery shopping and other errands. In his mid-50s he began to address his addictive behaviour, and he stopped much of the activity that had led him into trouble. At one point he attended a no-smoking clinic and ultimately succeeded in stopping smoking. He conquered his addictions in his own way and felt proud and confident of who he was.

In 2008, after several false starts with romantic relationships, he met a lovely lady named Jill who appreciated his many good traits, which had blossomed through the years. It was not long until he and Jill started to spend a lot of time together. They maintained their individual living quarters, and this seemed to give them space to develop their relationship slowly and thoughtfully. Lefty was finally able to invest in a loving and caring relationship.

The Group Home

1963 - 1964

Lefty 1963

Bob 1963

CHAPTER 3

BOB

December 28, 1963–January 12, 1964

S hortly after Lefty settled in, the police brought Bob to us in the middle of the night. We were told—and could see on the evening news—that there was a huge fire at one of Waterloo's downtown churches. Bob had been sighted there, so he was to remain with us until further evidence in the case was obtained and a decision was made about what to do with him. We welcomed Bob, just as we had Lefty.

He was a rough-looking, untidy 13-year-old from a low-rent housing development, the second-oldest of several children. The only identifying mark that one might notice was a nasty-looking scar on his right hand. He later told me that he had left some orange peels on the stove and so, as a punishment, his mother held his hand to the hot element.

He also told me that after he and his siblings were asleep at night, his parents would leave for an evening of drinking. When they returned, they would wake the older children with beatings. Bob seemed to be a favourite target, although he was not able to figure out why his parents would wake him, much less why they beat him.

During Bob's brief stay, no family members called or asked to visit him; he was alone. However, from the time he walked through the front door, he was compliant and cheerful—and happy to take a bath! When my in-laws arrived for Sunday dinner, he greeted them as his own, taking their coats and making sure they were comfortable. And oh, did he enjoy their compliments.

Bob and Lefty bonded almost immediately, and despite the fact that their lives later took completely different directions, they made it a point to see each other from time to time, continuing their brotherhood long after they left our home.

As it turned out, Bob was with us for only two weeks—and those days were filled with visits to the police for interviews and assessments. But each day he would return to our home, and that seemed to be a comfort to him. I had no opportunity to be involved in the legal proceedings, but I truly believed Bob could do well if they left him with us. However, the powers that be felt he was a threat to the community, and so he had to go to training school—a provincial school for children who could not be managed at home or in the community. There were several provincial schools. Some were in the countryside, with minimum security, while others were surrounded by tall barbed-wire fences, and the care was very rigid. Bob's was to be the latter.

Bob had been a model boy during his two weeks with us, and I did not feel that he would benefit from such an environment. However, my opinion was not considered. I cried a lot the day he left—and rightly so. The first week in training school he lost one of his front teeth in a fight. Soon after, he started his real education in crime.

There was nowhere for Bob to go during Christmas breaks and other holidays, and so the authorities would call and ask us to take him in. That was fine with us, and everyone was glad to see him. On Christmas Day, he would always ask to go to visit his biological family, and Evan would drive him over, but within 20 minutes we'd get a call from Bob, asking to be picked up again. He always tried—and it never worked. Whatever feelings he might have had he just tucked away, acting as though everything were fine. But over time we saw the heavy price he paid for doing that.

I don't remember how long Bob was in training school, but while he was there, I wrote him regularly. One day, I decided to send him a care package, just as I thought I might do someday for any of my kids who might be away at school or college. Boy, sweet innocence! It still surprises me how mature I could be in many instances and yet so naïve in others. Today, as a grandmother, I am known for the voluminous care packages I send to my grandchildren when they are away at school. So too did I create a wonderful box for Bob. He never wrote to thank me, but I just let that pass. Today I realize what a great party the institutional staff must have had with all those goodies.

Sometime after he was released from training school, Bob went to live in Toronto. There he got into drugs, and life became a fog for him. He decided to move farther west because he thought this was the thing to do, and along the way he developed a new way to support himself by writing cheques wherever he went. Once when Bob was in court for charges, the judge noted that he did not do anything violent, but that he was a very good con artist. That did not stop him, however, and the charges against him mounted to the point where he might have been sentenced to jail for the rest of his life. Instead, he was sentenced to a concurrent period of three years. The most devastating part of it all for Bob was that he spent his thirtieth birthday in jail, and that during his entire imprisonment he had only one visitor.

Once he was released, Bob moved back east and worked a variety of jobs. Although he took training at the local community college, he never managed to finish his courses.

Sometime after that, he met and then married a single mother,

Mary. Being a stepparent can be challenging for anyone, but Bob never adjusted to her three children, nor they to him. It was not long before he and Mary had their own daughter, Annabelle.

Her birth was a wonderful event for Bob, but it was also very stressful. Balancing the two family segments soon became impossible, and so the couple separated, with Mary taking primary custody and Bob having the baby every other weekend. Despite the difficulties in his own life, Bob was a good dad. He brought Annabelle to our home frequently, and they came for many of the special family occasions where there were other young children.

Annabelle was raised speaking French in her mother's home, and she attended a francophone school. Bob did not speak French, which posed an additional challenge as he tried to be part of his daughter's life. He taught Annabelle to speak English, and although she had some problems through the years, she has grown up to be a very nice young woman. She copes with some developmental issues, but she presents well socially and is very proud of the work she is able to do.

As with the training courses he took, Bob attended many addiction programs but had difficulty following through. He was up, and then he was down. But always he managed to pick himself up and start over again.

He had a habit of asking me for money, however, and over the years it became a huge issue. As he did with the cheques in Alberta, he would con me into helping him. And I was indeed conned. He would cry, telling me he would be beaten up if I didn't help him, and I knew very well it was because of drugs. Still, I did not want him to be hurt, so in the end I would give in—and then I would be mad at myself.

Following each incident, I would try to talk with Bob rationally about my inability and unwillingness to continue to respond to his heart-wrenching requests. Then one day, I lost it. I screamed and yelled and told him to go home—I did not want him to ask me for money again. Of course, I felt bad afterward, but I had had enough. Several months later, we discussed the issue, and I asked him what it was that made him finally understand that I could not and would not give him the money he asked for. He looked at me calmly and said, "You screamed at me, and then I knew you really meant it!" All those calm discussions meant nothing to him.

Early in 1990, Bob decided it was time to go on disability. He was able to present his case successfully to his doctor, who in turn signed the appropriate papers for his allowance. Unable to secure reasonable employment and trying to adjust to disability, he fell back into addictive behaviour, which complicated his life once more. He resumed the cycle of falling apart and then starting all over again.

Throughout these years, Bob did maintain his connection with us, helping with odd jobs around the house, although there were more and more days he could not come because of his increasing health issues. He was regularly hospitalized, but there never seemed to be a clear diagnosis. His loneliness and isolation would develop into severe pain and dehydration—a cycle that was repeated on a monthly basis. The hospital became Bob's home, and the attending staff his family, giving him the attention he needed.

CHAPTER 4

JOHNNY

February–December 1964

S oon after Bob left, Johnny arrived. He was barely 13 years old and the youngest of any of the boys who came to stay with us. He was also the youngest in his family. He was clearly troubled, acting out in the community in a variety of ways. His mother was unable to manage him, and his father was not around to help.

Johnny was with us for nine months, and he was by far the most difficult to deal with. He did not have friends in school, and he struggled academically. He was also a bed wetter, which was particularly challenging when it came time for him to go to summer camp. We worked on that issue with a system of positive reinforcement, and ultimately he was able to enjoy two weeks away with other children.

There was one significant event with Johnny that taught us all something about the conflict and confusion these children experience in their relationships. A neighbour was visiting, and we were having coffee in the kitchen when Johnny rushed in the door and went straight to his bedroom—"to rest," he said. Within minutes, we heard screaming and wailing from outside.

It was a 12-year-old neighbour girl from down the street. Blood was streaming from her mouth, and it was clear she needed to go to the hospital. Her mother and another neighbour took her. When I asked Johnny if he knew what had happened, his response was an innocent-looking no, which indicated yes to me. Sometime later that evening, the mother of the little girl came to see me, claiming that Johnny had bitten her daughter in the mouth. They had been playing together nicely, she said, and there was no quarrel, but he had bitten her. The bite required five stitches.

Later that evening I spoke to Johnny again, but he denied everything. After a little quiet talking together, he acknowledged that maybe he did bite her, but he did not know why. So we talked a bit more, and then we walked down the street together to say sorry to the girl and her mother. We worked it out with them.

The following month at the CAS meeting, I brought the incident up with the consulting psychiatrist, Dr. Hunt. The lively discussion that ensued was very interesting and enlightening. After reviewing the circumstances, Dr. Hunt hypothesized that Johnny may have leaned forward to kiss his friend, but then, in a moment of panic and uncertainty, he bit her instead. Think about it.

One of the things that Johnny enjoyed was going to the stockyards on Saturdays to see the animals. There was also a flea market there, and one day he came home with a sexy red bathing suit he had purchased for his mother. He was so proud of it; he slept with it every night for weeks, until he had the opportunity to give it to her. He was disappointed that she would not model it for him, but she was very sensitive to his intent, and she did thank him for it.

Johnny stayed with us until the end of our project. At that point, my 15-year-old sister had come to live with us, and she and Johnny did not get along well. Because she was my sister, I felt I had to consider her needs first. So when the CAS asked if we would continue having Johnny even after the group home project was completed, I had to say no. I felt that his problems needed to be dealt with at a much more significant level, and that was not something I was able to offer at the time. I had my husband, my daughter, Trisha, and my sister to consider, and I was also expecting our second baby.

I felt very bad about my decision, and I still think of Johnny often. He went on to another foster home, and just a couple of days later he phoned me. I had to encourage him to try hard to make it work, although I knew that would be difficult for him to do.

Several years later, I heard that Johnny was in jail. Lefty had seen him there, and we agreed that he would not have managed well in jail. His regular life was difficult enough for him. I don't know where Johnny is now, but I still worry about him.

CHAPTER 5

VAL

March–May 1964

A new boy was added to our household in the spring of 1964. Val was the oldest of three children in his family, and it was unclear to me why he had been taken away from his home. Surely the CAS had this information, but they didn't share it with me. Val had a stocky build, a smallish head and a grin that made you wonder what was going to happen next. Quick to argue, he often picked fights with the other two boys.

Val was a child of few words, but his behaviour was always attention-seeking. He would walk past the kitchen table, pick up the sugar bowl and drink from it as if it were a glass of water. I had to be constantly on the alert as to where he was, who he was with and what he was doing.

Managing three boys at one time became increasingly difficult for me. And then one morning I came down the stairs and caught sight of Val in the living room, taking a swipe at my young daughter. It was not a hard slap, but that was it for me. I could not risk her safety.

After a quick consultation with the social worker, Perry Max, and another with Dr. Hunt, plans were made for Val to move out of our home immediately. I don't know why, but it was decided that Val would return to his own family. Before he left, I had a little talk with him. He knew why he had to leave, but I told him that I was sorry we could not have been more helpful to him. I also told him that I hoped his experience away from home would help him settle back more easily with his family. Maybe he could do things differently, I said. He said nothing. It was a funny kind of good-bye. The other boys never spoke of him after that.

In light of that experience, especially, it might seem strange that I did not have more concern about the kind of children we welcomed into our home—their backgrounds, that is, and why they came to us. However, the group home concept at that time was very basic: to provide a safe place for children in difficulty so that they did not have to go to adult institutions. Social agencies did not have the knowledge then that they have today, and I was given very little information about the boys' backgrounds. However, I did have access to immediate help when necessary because we were part of the pilot project. So when there was a situation with Val that put our daughter in danger, action was taken and the problem resolved immediately.

Four years after we had the group home, a very interesting thing happened. It was a warm evening, and we had just returned from our summer cottage at Lac Sam. I had put six-year-old Trisha and her younger brother to bed and was doing the usual unpacking and sorting. There was a knock at the door, and when I opened it, there stood Val; he had come for a visit and a chat. I welcomed him in and poured some lemonade, and we went out on the porch to talk. For a whole hour I sat and listened while he talked nonstop about school, home and all the things that were going on in his life. He was animated and seemed happy. And then he thanked me for all that I had done for him. He was fine now, he said. Then he got up and left. I never heard from him again.

What had I done? Very little, it seemed to me. Was it making him face the consequences of swatting a little girl? Or was it the short talk I had with him before he left? Perhaps it just felt really good to get back home. I will never really know, but the important thing is that Val seemed to be doing well in life. I want to assume that he continues to do so.

CHAPTER 6

DAN

July–October 1964

J ohnny was a leader when it came to mischief, and unfortunately he was able to influence our next boy, Dan, who was a follower.

When Dan joined us, there was not as much fanfare as there had been with Bob, but it was another case of pyromania—only on a much lesser scale. He had been caught at the scene of several small fires because his habit was to return to watch them.

Dan was a cheery, chatty lad of 14, the youngest of three boys in his family. By the time he arrived at our home, the CAS had begun giving me a little more background on the boys. There were two interesting dynamics in Dan's situation: First, one of his older brothers had severe psychological problems, which took a fair amount of their parents' time and attention. Second, the parents had marital problems, and Dan was regularly pulled into the middle of them. He often acted as the peacemaker, siding with his mother and trying to protect her, so he served a useful purpose although it was difficult for him. This role reversal meant there was no one for him to turn to when he had a problem.

Despite his troubled background, Dan settled into our home very easily, and he and Lefty managed well together. And although he had never had any sisters, he treated Trisha as his younger sibling.

Dan was with us for three and a half months. During that time he attended his regular school, where he played the trumpet in the school band. He was doing well, but as he and Johnny spent a lot of time together, I knew I had to keep my eye on them. It turned out that my instincts were correct; there were two significant events to follow.

The first happened one afternoon, when Johnny and Dan decided to make use of our neighbour's plum tree that was laden with ripe fruit. They picked a couple of plums, and what began as a game of catch developed into a contest of throwing plums against the neighbour's stucco wall.

Fortunately, there were only a couple of small windows on that side of the house. Still, by the time we discovered what was going on, the tree was almost bare and the wall was dripping purple! I was thankful that Evan took over and supervised the hosing and scrubbing. It took hours.

Then it was my job to take the boys to confess and apologize for their transgressions. Luckily, the neighbours were a mellow older couple, and having had a large family themselves, they showed some appreciation for the temptation that led to the disaster. They were very accommodating.

Although there were issues with Johnny and Dan, we always managed to work them out—until the one time they went too far. Remember, Dan was a great kid in many ways, but he also was easily led, and Johnny was able to lead him. So one day, probably bored, the two of them found themselves near the railroad crossing and decided to tinker with the signals. To this day, I do not know if they understood the significance of what they were doing.

Once again the police were at our door. This was a very serious issue, and the investigation led to charges and then to court. Perry Max, the social worker, came to pick up the boys and take them to court. Dan was quiet; Johnny, on the other hand, was very excited. He told me not to worry about him and suggested that I would be able to watch him on television, just as we watched those other court programs.

The outcome was not a happy one for me. Dan, the follower, was sent away to training school for 14 months. This was a closed and monitored environment somewhat like a children's jail. The severity of the term was based on the previous convictions that had brought him to us in the first place. Johnny, the leader, was deemed to be too immature to understand the gravity of what he'd done. Consequently it was decided that he should remain with us.

Once out of training school, Dan returned to his own home, where he lived for the next 35 years until it was time for his parents to move into seniors' accommodations. Each parent took up a separate residence.

So at age 53, Dan got his first apartment. This new lifestyle proved to be very agreeable to him, and he began to wonder why he had not made the move many years before. He and his parents continued to have a meal together once a week, and they enjoyed each other's company in these situations.

When his mother passed away, Dan continued to see his dad and began to try to understand the past and enhance their present relationship. He had a group of good friends who cared about him and were very supportive of his interests.

I had a couple of visits from Dan over the years, but generally my only communication from him was a card at Christmas, simply signed, "Dan Q."

Lefty, Bob and Trisha   Christmas 1964

Lefty, Trisha and Bob   1971

Lefty 1977

Dan 1977

Airdrie with Bob at his wedding   1985

Annabelle celebrating with Bob on his birthday

CHAPTER 7

AIRDRIE

1963–65

Our year with the boys was filled with activity and adventure. It gave me a rich opportunity to understand some of the human dynamics that I would later deal with in my career. We never had more than three boys at a time in our home, and even at that, they typically were not with us for long. The interesting observation for me was the bond that developed between the boys even though their time together was brief.

The Children's Aid Society had one social worker from the agency to monitor the activities and progress of our boys for the year that the project was run. Once a month, the CAS staff would meet to present difficult cases to a consulting psychiatrist. During the year of our pilot project, I was the presenter each month, and this gave everyone a chance to note problems and sometimes progress with our boys. The input I received was very helpful to me. I was often weary at the beginning of the presentation, but the lively and insightful discussion that followed and Dr. Hunt's wise words usually gave me renewed energy to return home and carry on.

Life in our house was typical of that of a larger family where common sense had to prevail and specific events had logical consequences. We welcomed each boy readily, incorporating them into the family with little discussion of why they were with us. In general, things ran fairly smoothly when Evan and I were at home. If we wanted to go out for an evening, we got a sitter—and that was almost always a disaster. The boys would become very disruptive. In fact, no sitter we retained would ever come back—not psychology students, friends or anyone else we prevailed upon. We did not get out much.

After the year was up, it was time for me to move on with my own life and family. We moved to a smaller home. Some of the boys did keep in touch with us, but they knew that they could visit only if they were not in difficulty with the law and not involved with anything illegal. They respected these boundaries, just as they had in our home.

Between 1965 and 1970, my own life took a turn. After my second child, Graham, was born, I realized once again that it was necessary for me to get a job outside the home. I did not go back to the CAS but rather answered an ad for a position at the outpatient department of psychiatry at our local hospital.

I went to the interview but quickly realized that they wanted someone with a bachelor's degree in social work. The fact that I had young children did not seem to pose a problem anymore, but now my formal education was not adequate.

Oh well. The social worker and I had a polite chat, anyway, and then she asked if I would like to meet the head psychiatrist, just to say hello. That was fine with me.

Dr. Monk was a slight, balding man with a serious expression. When I walked into his office, his hands were folded on his pristine desk, but he rose to greet me in a friendly manner. Within minutes we were engaged in a lively discussion; he seemed particularly interested in my experiences in Montreal and Toronto. I alluded to the fact that I had worked with foster children as well.

After quite a long discussion, I got up to leave, as I knew my degree did not meet the job requirements. I actually had my hand on the doorknob when he seemed to realize the connection.

"Are you the one who had the group home?" he asked.

"Yes."

"Come back and sit down."

As we resumed our talk, it became clear that Dr. Monk knew quite a bit about what I had done. In fact, unbeknownst to me, he had seen most of the boys for assessment over the year. The boys regularly went out to appointments, but I was not always told what they were about.

"Well," Dr. Monk said, "that makes quite a difference. When would you like to start?"

And so began the next stage of my life. I worked for a year half-time, which was just perfect with me. Then, because there was a new school of social work opening in the fall, Dr. Monk suggested it might be wise for me to apply, but the school was taking full-time students only. I was somewhat discouraged; I had hoped to take just one or two courses at a time because of the children. So I decided to take the summer to think about what I should do. You can imagine how surprised I was soon afterward to receive a letter telling me I had been accepted for full-time study that fall.

My emotions were mixed. How would I possibly manage? But manage you do. My father stepped forward and offered to pay a nanny to care for the children—but then there were the school fees. Fortunately, Evan worked at the university, so I had to pay only half the standard fees. To cover that, I applied for a mental health grant. In short order I received a letter telling me that I had been turned down for financial assistance because I was married and had children. *Not again!* I thought.

Realizing that I was always going to have to be gainfully employed,

I wrote back to explain that *because* I was married and had two children, it was necessary for me to work—and so I needed a grant. This time I was successful. In 1968, I earned my master's in social work from Waterloo Lutheran University (now Wilfrid Laurier University).

Throughout this time, Lefty was living in Waterloo and continued to stay in touch and even enjoy some outings with the children. He was very protective of them.

As he and the other boys moved into early adulthood, each going in a different direction, they had to bump up against the changes taking place in my life—because, like everyone, I had my own issues. As life would have it, once I was self-sufficient, Evan decided to leave his full-time job to pursue a life in theatre. He also decided that after eight years of marriage, he did not want to continue to carry family responsibilities.

We separated, and later I moved to Ottawa as a single mom with two children. I was the sole provider for the family for nine years.

In retrospect, I wondered how that dramatic change in my life affected Lefty, Bob and Dan, who had come from disrupted families to be placed in a stable family setting. After all the hard work we had shared, had my actions been damaging to them—exploding the myth of good family relationships and a sense of belonging? At the time I didn't have the opportunity to think about it, but when we all gathered together later, I dared to ask them. Their response was unanimous: I had done the right thing in moving forward on my own with my children. We were still a family, they said, only in a different form.

Life continued to evolve, and my family constellation grew yet again. I met and four years later married Jack, a father of three, and we joined our families into one household with five children, aged 12, 13, 14, 15, and 16. Some of "the boys" were included in the happy celebration: Lefty and Dan came to our wedding. Bob was in jail.

Chapter 8

❦

The Reunion

2009

L ife continued with sporadic visits, phone calls and Christmas cards from the boys. Everyone grew up in his or her own way. Thirty-three years after our marriage, when Jack passed away after a long struggle with dementia, my biological family were present with love and concern, and my stepchildren, too, were very helpful and caring. My foster children came forward in their own ways as part of our larger family circle.

Lefty called regularly to offer his comfort. And after many years of simply signing his Christmas card "Dan Q.," Dan wrote a beautiful letter acknowledging my loss. Bob, who had moved to Ottawa, was right there to help. How blessed is that! We were together as a family again, but now I was the one being cared for.

The first Christmas after Jack's passing, Bob phoned me, sounding very excited. It was still a week before the twenty-fifth, and Bob usually came to share the holiday with us, but he could not wait for Christmas Day—he had to come by immediately. And so he did. He arrived with a large, beautifully wrapped box.

"Open it!" he said. There was a gleam in his eye, and his face lit up with pure joy.

It was a lovely food mixer—Bob had remembered my little hand-held mixer, whose cord repeatedly fell out. It was irritating, to say the least, but somehow I never managed to replace it. Well! Now I had a big, beautiful, new stand-up mixer with a secure plug. I was thrilled and very touched—and Bob was grinning from ear to ear.

And then another door opened when Dan decided to come visit me. The time was right, and we suggested to Lefty that he might come too. All we needed was Bob to complete the circle for three of the boys—a get-together 47 years after the pilot project. The three had not all lived with me at the same time, yet there seemed to be a kinship among them, a brotherhood created by each having travelled through the door of our group home when they were teens. Now that they were men in their 60s, I wondered what they would remember and how they would react to all being together in one space for the first time.

We decided to get together for three days. Lefty and Dan would travel to Ottawa by train and stay with me at my home. Bob lived in Ottawa, so he would stay at his own place. As a precaution, I gave my neighbours advance notice of the visit. "I know that I am a relatively new widow," I said. "I am going to have three men at my place for the weekend. They are my boys, and I don't want any gossip."

When I met and greeted Lefty and Dan at the station, the reality of the present instantly melted back to those first days when I knew them as young teens. Lefty was taller and somewhat slimmer than I remembered, and he was dressed in what he considered to be current travel mode, with earplugs and wires keeping him in touch with his music. Dan, on the other hand, had gained a concerning amount of weight, but he still had a cheery disposition that lit up his face. They looked at me and in unison cried, "Please, please, please, can we stop at

Timmy's for coffee before we go home?" I knew my boys were home—
and that there was a lot to discover ahead of us.

And so it unfolded: three days of revelation. Lots of laughter,
many never-before-told stories, many retold stories and the discovery
that we all had had a lifetime of experience in the years spanning our
shared home and our senior-hood. Much had been learned. The men
acknowledged that there still were things I should never be told, but
there were many stories I would learn about and enjoy. It had been 47
years since we first met. Who has the luxury of that kind of diary—an
almost 50-year-long record of what really happens to a child when life
is not fair to him in his early years?

I cooked for the boys all weekend, and then they decided to treat
me to dinner. Dan asked me to get dressed up, and so I did.

Over dinner, Dan made some interesting observations. "Sometimes
when you have a positive experience," he said, "it may not solve
everything, and you may continue to make more mistakes, but you
still draw on that experience."

He said he had told his friends he was "going to visit an older
lady—a professional lady," adding, "I brag about you. I brag with pride."
He said he had never been friends with anyone as long as he had with
Lefty and me.

Dan seemed happy with his lot in life. He sometimes wished for
companionship, but he also cherished his singleness. In hindsight, he
said, he felt he had a subconscious distrust that coloured his relationships;
there had been only conflict, not problem-solving, in his household for
the first 45 years of his life. When asked why he did not leave his parents'
home, he said he did not make enough money and didn't think he could
manage on his own. He had watched his older brother go through many
psychiatric problems and one failed marriage with a wife who had no
respect for him. The picture of his brother carrying two jobs, yet going

further into debt trying to support two children, was a grim vignette for Dan. His brother finally walked away, and eventually had a second, better marriage, but he died of cancer at age 54.

Today, Dan does not drink, do drugs or smoke, and he uses the money he once would have spent on those things to reward himself. He has travelled Canada coast-to-coast five times, and he takes the occasional trip to Toronto, where he stays in a nice hotel and attends a theatrical production. Dan has always loved music and is conversant with a variety of musical and literary subjects, both modern and classical. There is joy in his voice when he talks and jokes, and he readily acknowledges his pride in having moved his own life forward.

Lefty kept in touch with me through good times and bad. In later years, as he tried to reconnect with his daughter, Summer, he regularly called to ask for guidance on specific issues. It seemed our most important conversation was the one confronting his need to become a better listener. He was thrilled with the resulting shift in their relationship. Now he understood and respected the fact that Summer had a busy life, and he was able to appreciate that she had to make her own decisions.

At the age of 47, Lefty found out that he had a learning disability and was suffering from depression. Initial counselling did not help him. He then was referred to a day treatment program that helped him understand how his disability—and adults' reaction to it—affected his life from a young age. He learned that he was not stupid or lazy, but that he had dyslexia, a genetic disorder that prevents the brain from transforming thought into action.

It was such a relief for Lefty to know that bad things did not happen because he was a bad person. Now that he understood his special needs, he was able to use a government program to complete high school and go on to study gerontology. His placement was in a nursing home, and he enjoyed the work tremendously, taking great pride in his accomplishments and feeling confident to seriously enter the workforce. Of great importance was the fact that his own mom was so proud of him at graduation. He felt that his dad would have been proud too.

When Lefty spoke of his work with seniors, he described how their eyes lit up when he walked into the room. He was very proud of the contribution he was making in their lives.

Lefty and Dan shared their stories openly and happily during this visit, laughing and feeling very comfortable together. Dan said he had never been able to talk with his parents, but in an accepting environment he expressed himself easily.

Bob was part of the threesome, but through all the storytelling, quips and laughter, he sat solemnly and uneasily. From time to time he would put his head in his hands. When we asked him to share his stories, he claimed he tried not to remember the past because it was too horrendous. Indeed, he had talked with me for many hours over the years about the bad things that had happened, and I knew he often tried to reach out to his siblings and sometimes his father. They never responded.

As with the other boys, there were long periods when I would not hear from Bob, but then he would return from wherever he had been to try to start his life over. Many times I had watched him try to climb out of his addictions. He would succeed for weeks, sometimes months, sometimes years—but the cycle always resumed eventually. Now, however, he seemed to have finally overcome the alcohol, drugs, gambling and even smoking, having been clean for several years. Like the others, he enjoyed taking pride in what he was able to do and give. So why now—why at this point of the reunion—was Bob so withdrawn and uncomfortable?

There had been a strong sense of brotherhood among the boys— each relationship having developed in its own way. Lefty and Bob had a long history together, while Dan's liberation from his parents' home helped him reconnect with Lefty decades after they left the group home. But at this crucial point, when all three of them had indicated that a get-together was in order—it was arranged at their request—Bob was odd man out. He had wanted to participate in the reunion, or so he had said, but now he seemed emotionally paralyzed.

There had been three major losses in Bob's life recently. Each loss was important, but it took me a while to realize their significance. Three months before Jack died, Bob's father-in-law died suddenly. Bob had enjoyed a good relationship with his father-in-law; he looked after his in-laws' grounds and did house repairs for them, much as he did for us. I think he learned a great deal from both Jack and his father-in-law, looking up to them as important models and reaping the benefits of their positive feedback.

About three months after Jack's death, Bob's own father died. He had been unwell for many years, during which time Bob had tried to work out a relationship with him, but it was difficult. So when Bob learned that his father was seriously ill and in hospital, he drove a significant distance to see him. He arrived 15 minutes too late. His father had passed away.

There was no funeral for Bob's father and no way for Bob to grieve with other family members. And so there he was, having lost the three most important men in his life within a very brief period of time.

I didn't see Bob again until two months after the reunion, when he was in hospital for what seemed to be a longstanding medical problem. I went to visit him, and he almost immediately broke down and told me he was on drugs again. I had to think about that carefully, because earlier, when the four of us had spent three days sharing together—seeming to understand the different yet similar dynamics of the boys' respective lives—none of us had recognized what was happening to

Bob. With his very minimal participation, the only thing that was clear was that Bob did not want to talk about his family with the other boys present. He was that capable of hiding his addiction from us, deflecting the present onto the past.

My first reaction was, "Bob, you skewed my statistics!" I truly believed that after all the years of turmoil, all three boys had finally managed to turn their lives around. But then there was reality.

Not long after our visit, Dan's mother passed away. While Dan was dealing with his grief, he was also using his time to get to know his dad more intimately. He told me he wishes he had been treated better in his younger years, but he added that it's too easy to blame others for life's ills. He consciously tries to treat others well.

After our three days together, I had a positive feeling about Dan, who was sustaining his new and active life. Within a few months, Lefty was in a loving, fulfilling relationship. Bob was attending AA once again and renewing his relationship with his mother-in-law by playing bridge, doing grounds work for her and attending church at her request. He also was helpful to me when I needed a hand. Things seemed stable for all three of them. Yet deceit also kept Bob going for a while. The judge had been right: he was a good con man.

Getting together after 47 years   May 2010

Dan, Lefty and Bob   Lots of food

Bob, Airdrie, Dan and Lefty   Over to dinner   May 2010

Lefty and Dan   Ready to catch the train home

CHAPTER 9

CONTEMPLATION

I spent the next several months after our reunion concentrating on the real outcome of the group home—what was really accomplished and learned. I took the opportunity to escape to a warm climate to mull it all over. While I was away, I received a most unexpected phone call: Lefty had been found dead in his bed; apparently, he had suffered a heart attack. He had had one a year before and been hospitalized, but he seemed perfectly healthy when I saw him in the spring. His death was a great shock to me.

In inquiring further, I learned that his love, Jill, had had a stroke two months earlier and as a result had moved back to her family's home so that they could look after her. What a great loss for both of them. I had to wonder about the dynamics of their situation, and whether Jill's illness and departure somehow led to Lefty's demise.

Despite the shock and loss, I had a warm sense of satisfaction that Lefty had managed to work out most of his issues before he died. Perhaps most important, he had become a father again to Summer, and he had found a special relationship with Jill.

Summer and Lefty's siblings held a very touching memorial for him at the seniors' home across the street from his apartment. Lefty's friends, neighbours and associates attended, and he was truly honoured and appreciated for who he was. Bob managed to borrow some money so that he could attend the funeral as well. It was clear that Lefty's death was a great loss to him, but as was his nature, he did not talk about it.

Six months later there was an interment, which I was able to attend. It was a beautiful day, and we all lingered by the graveside, sharing memories. That afternoon we gathered back at Summer's home, where I gave her the beautiful little watch on a gold chain her dad had given to me so many years before.

I had not seen Lefty's younger brother and sister for almost 40 years, and now here they were, with their own grown children. As we sat on the balcony overlooking the spacious acreage at Summer's home, Lefty's sister turned to me and asked, "So how did you decide to become a foster mother, Airdrie?"

"I didn't decide that," I answered. "It just happened. It was only for one year of my life, but it turned out to be a gift forever."

Each of the five boys had his own path. They showed up at my door with many of the same issues, notably family dysfunction, acting out and seemingly feeling that they didn't belong anywhere. I don't think any of them felt respected or understood. And I don't think even they realized what was missing in their lives to make them feel unhappy.

When we consider the costs and benefits of incarceration, therapy, pharmacology and the operation of government agencies, many hours and many dollars are invested in troubled children, often with only a limited return. It may be that some of the simple components of life, such as recognition, caring and the establishment of meaningful boundaries, should play a far more significant part in society's approach to these children.

Let me acknowledge the many happy success stories there are about foster children and group homes today. They are encouraging as we seek to continue a scheme of care that can heal and enrich the lives of some children. There are, however, still too many situations where children's real needs are not met or children slip through the cracks of society. I have often wondered whether we truly understand how long it might take to accomplish peace of mind and wholeness of body. Can we know who will heal—or who cannot heal?

I fell into this experience by chance, and initially it was not entirely for all the right reasons. I needed a job. I also did not have extensive experience to take on such an important project. Nevertheless, it turned out to be one of the most precious times in my life, allowing me to contribute positively to five other young lives.

Furthermore, it was some of the very best "training by chance" that I ever received, which held me in good stead for the 45-year career in counselling and family therapy that followed. An internship of this kind would greatly enhance anyone's preparation to work with children and their families.

CHAPTER 10

CONCLUSION

T his is a story set in 1963. While times have changed over the ensuing 48 years, the issues involved in managing and caring for troubled children remain the same. Although I have not worked directly in the child welfare system for many years now, I have certainly stayed current with its dilemmas, first through my work in a community hospital department of psychiatry in Kitchener, Ontario (1966–72), and then as director of social work at the Children's Hospital of Eastern Ontario (1974–85), where I maintained a strong administrative link with the Children's Aid Society. Through my subsequent private practice (1988–2010), I used CAS as a resource for some of my cases. There was also a group home in my own community.

Throughout those years, there have always been issues that I felt should have been addressed. Children's needs really must be taken care of without shuffling the children from home to home to home because of their behaviour. Investing in these troubled children is costly, and unfortunately, many politicians and leaders do not recognize the benefit of addressing issues early rather than paying the long-term price for the many difficult years of life to follow.

Almost 50 years later I have posed these concerns to professionals who are in the field today. The responses vary from "Yes, that is what we do today," to "There is no time" or "There is no budget." When you're dealing with human beings—young people who are still in the process of being moulded and guided, and, more important, who often have not had a fair start in life—it seems only proper to reexamine these issues and try to establish acceptable and productive parameters for their care.

Each of the boys placed with us was let down by the system in some ways, and each had things that went well. Perhaps we can learn from what happened to them and improve things for the next generation.

Lefty
***

During the six months Lefty was with us, his mother visited on three occasions. There were never any telephone calls from siblings or other family members. I like to believe that because his stay with us was without incident, because he was aging out of CAS care, and perhaps because the agency wanted to place another boy in our home, the decision was made to send Lefty back to his parents.

That move happened with no specific plan at our end or theirs. Lefty was happy to return home because his dad, who had not had any contact with him during the six-month period, promised him a car. That did not materialize.

CAS may have had a plan on paper regarding Lefty's return home, but if so, I didn't see it. Ideally, such a plan would have included a visit home after he was placed with us, which would have helped his later reintegration into his own family flow smoothly and in a welcoming fashion. Lefty needed to feel that he was one of them again. What he did instead was to visit his "brothers" at our home, where he knew he fit in. He was cheated, but then again his family was too.

Fortunately, through therapy and his own self-development, and also through the maturing and resolve of his family, Lefty was finally able to enjoy them, at least in part. This achievement took years of therapy, education and government money—and the ability to like and respect himself, which was necessary for his ultimate happiness.

Better action on Lefty's behalf and interaction with his family during his placement might well have benefited Lefty, his family and ultimately society.

Bob

***

Bob was with us for just two weeks. During that brief time there were never any calls or visits from his family, nor did he try to contact them.

Bob's life has been a roller coaster, typical of many children who have suffered abuse and neglect. He has tried repeatedly and without success to reconnect with various family members. While he may have been somewhat clumsy and assuming in his efforts, I wonder if his family's unresponsiveness stemmed from a presumption that Bob had been bad and therefore had been "taken away." His was a very complex family. Perhaps if they had been invited to discuss the plan for Bob's placement, they might have been more open to his return. It would have helped to put him in a positive environment where he could realistically be expected to succeed rather than a punitive one that offered him no hope for a future. Ideally, Bob should have been kept in a family setting—such as the group home—where he could experience reasonable expectations and positive reinforcement. A secure or locked training school environment could not provide this.

Bob continues to struggle each day. His challenge at present is the diagnosis of cancer. For all the risks he has taken with his life, this reality has been devastating to him. When he received his diagnosis, he once again reached out to two of his sisters. Initially they showed some concern, and one said she would try to visit him. Bob was very happy and looked forward to the possibility, but neither sister came to visit, and there was no further communication. Once again he was let down.

When I visited Bob in his apartment, he told me in a straightforward fashion that he had discussed with his doctor the fact that he was continuing to smoke cigarettes and marijuana. This new openness has eased his relationship with the doctor, who is now providing medication to address his addiction. It seems that now, confronted by this serious illness, Bob has been able to show his real and truthful self.

Fortunately, there is a blessing in Bob's life: his relationship with his daughter and her boyfriend, who seem to be teaching Bob the joys of working steadily, as well as having fun.

Johnny
***

Of all the boys who stayed with us, Johnny is the one I wish I had the opportunity to plan for again. He was with us for the longest period, and his abilities were the most limited. Yet he had a likeable side that might have helped him along in life if he had had a better understanding of even a few little things.

My life situation, not Johnny's, was the reason he had to move on to another foster home. And I think he could have understood that if it had been explained properly to him. From his perception, not only was he replaced by my sister, but he was also replaced, so to speak, by a new baby—and another boy, at that.

I regret that even with my busy schedule, I did not accompany Johnny on his pre-placement visit to his new setting. It was never suggested. Had I gone with him, I believe that I could have given him a more positive perspective of the move. In hindsight, I also think it would have been wise to invite Johnny back to our house to meet the new baby. He had lived with us through my pregnancy, and he might have enjoyed the outcome, even if only for a short visit. I think that might have given him a better understanding of why he had to move.

I feel certain that Johnny was one of many children who get shunted from one foster home to another. I have to wonder if they truly understand why they are being moved, or whether the experiences become just a prolonged blur of rejection.

This leads to a significant point: the needs of both the foster child and the foster family must be taken into account. In Johnny's case, we were the ones whose situation had changed. It was not Johnny's behaviour that led to the change. That sort of shifting of needs is, in itself, important for everyone involved to understand.

Val

***

Val was with us for only a brief six weeks. While his behaviour was generally difficult to deal with and he did not integrate with the other boys, he made just one mistake that had to be dealt with directly: he hit two-year-old Trisha. Our decision to remove Val from our home was not instantaneous, nor was it made in anger. We had to go through the proper channels to make a suitable plan. There were logical consequences for his behaviour, and we discussed them with him quietly and calmly.

I am not certain why the decision was made to return Val to his parents, but I am very grateful for that. Had he simply been moved to another foster home, he could easily have become a casualty of his own negative behaviour and, therefore, many moves.

The fact that he returned several years later to say thank you strengthens my belief in the power of direct, fair, calm communication. Time is a huge factor in managing the cases of troubled children. However, it benefits us and them in the long term if we use every opportunity to comment on difficult issues. In this way we can try to pave the way for these young people so that the world makes more sense to them. We know that the early years of childhood are significant for learning, and we must persist through the difficult years of adolescence, believing that children continue to learn and to benefit from the acknowledgement of their importance.

Dan

***

Dan was a different story altogether. It would appear that despite significant family tensions, some of which may have stemmed from one sibling's severe behavioural and personality issues, there was probably an opportunity to welcome Dan at birth.

With stability and affection in his early years, and having been blessed with a cheery disposition, Dan wasn't responsible for his family's conflict—but he was caught in the crossfire. It's likely that his inability to manage or resolve the greater family issues caused him to act out in a very frightening manner, which escalated as they became a cry for help.

Dan's penchant for setting fires did not continue once he was out of the conflict, but his eagerness to please led to ill-advised activities, which in turn led to more serious consequences.

First he was removed from his family to the group home, and then he was removed from society, being sent to training school. In both instances, he moved on to a more secure environment. Those environments, combined with his own development and maturity, allowed him to grow into a more responsible lifestyle and integrate well into society, which reinforced his more positive and productive direction.

Newly grounded, he could begin to understand some of his family dynamics. As his parents aged and probably mellowed, he began to enjoy and appreciate them for who they were.

Dan is in control of his own life now, with a routine that is sound; he provides his own structure to ensure that his life is full and happy. When we last spoke, he was planning a trip to Newfoundland. The trip was a year out, but he already had his hotel and transportation reservations; he so benefits from the planning and the excitement of it all.

Dan has returned twice to see the training school where he stayed as a child. It was an open-concept school when he was there, but now it is an adult facility surrounded by a high barbed-wire fence. He understands why the school had certain rules and expectations; they allowed him to think beyond his reactionary behaviour. Dan's life, learning and activities today surely have made up for the restricted social education afforded him as a youth. He has taken his new strengths and used them to move forward on his own.

Recommendations

It would be quite easy for me to set out grandiose and costly recommendations for foster care that would undoubtedly end up on a shelf, gathering dust. They would be warranted and effective but not acceptable in today's reality of stringent budgets. The following, however, are some important parameters to consider for an effective and meaningful foster experience:

- Bigger is not better. A small group home, not to exceed four children with significant behavioural histories, will have a better chance of incorporating the children and giving them a positive family experience.

- It is important to admit one child at a time into the home to allow for an initial adjustment period, however brief. Each child needs to establish his own place within the family.

- Be aware of and acknowledge the history of the biological family, and build from there with the child. The child and his parents need to be part of the planning and treatment team if he is expected to return to his original home.

- Keep the door open to parents. Visiting helps ease the blow to self-esteem that they experience with the temporary loss of their child.

- Group home situations may be temporary, but they need to be grounding and welcoming experiences in order to help the foster children move forward with a sense of optimism. Today, we have treatment facilities to look after our most disturbed children. This enables foster homes to deal with very difficult but less severe cases.

- Without being intrusive, placement agencies should seek to understand the needs and special situations of the foster families so that appropriate placements can be made. This encourages a more positive response from the foster families themselves, thereby enhancing the level and availability of care.

- The foster family should be recognized as a valid and important family form in its own right. That recognition is important not just to foster children but also to the foster families, whose important role in society deserves greater awareness and appreciation.

John Bowlby, said to be the father of Attachment Theory, has examined and studied children from infancy to adolescence. In the mid '80s I had the privilege of spending part of a day with him at the Children's Hospital of Eastern Ontario. He was a gentle man with a deep concern for infants and young children. He spoke of the effects of sadness and loss on children in the early stages of life, and he stressed the importance of interaction to give young children a positive parent-child relationship which would, in turn, lead to a more secure child, with a greater opportunity for healthy psychological development.

More specifically, Bowlby felt that in order to grow mentally healthy, a child must experience a warm, intimate and continuous relationship with his mother or a mother substitute, where both could find satisfaction and enjoyment.

In our case, even though my family did not provide long-term foster care, in most of the cases a strong bond was established either from the boy to us or from us to the boy. That bond became a strong bridge that the boys could use to relate to me later in their lives.

In the same way, if a child's life is disrupted for any number of reasons, there must be a bridge made to the next stage of his life. He needs to understand why the change is happening (logical consequences), and he needs to be welcomed to the next stage with an understanding that he can participate in improving his own life situation.

Children also should be encouraged to verbalize their feelings of grief, loss, sadness and abandonment so that they can safely move forward with a sense of belonging. Without this process, it's likely that they will begin acting out, and a dangerous and unhappy lifestyle may result.

This leads me to consider the foster experience as a family form. Brief as the fostering stage might be, it can inject a new feeling of belonging. As Dan said, "Sometimes when you have a positive experience, it may not solve everything, and you may continue to make more mistakes, but you still draw on that experience."

Five boys: each with a different story, each with a different outcome.

Five men: each dealing with his own history, each grappling with the reality of his own life.

With these five lives we have almost 50 years of history to learn from so that a child tomorrow might be spared unnecessary pain when life fails to give him a fair chance in the world.

… AND AFTERWORD

Hi Airdrie,

I am sending a short note today just to express some feelings I have now. It seems now since you started this project a few years ago when you had Lefty, Bob and me at your home, I finally have come to realize that I want to make more of an effort to come and visit, if only once a year. It was nice to renew my friendship with Lefty about a year before our get-together and although I had never really crossed paths with Bob, it was nice to see him at your place.

With the passing of my mother and the passing of Lefty, both in the last year or so, I don't want to miss more opportunities to be with the people who are important to me. It seems now that

I am closer than ever to my father and brother, who too seems to be more open and receptive, and to you, Airdrie, while at times when I didn't keep in touch except for a yearly Christmas card, you always kept the door open and kept me informed of what was going on in your life. In hindsight, I would have liked to have gotten to know Jack more than I did.

I will close for now, Airdrie, and I look forward to reading your book when it comes out. It seemed therapeutic in a way, our get-togethers when you were putting everything together! It brought back a lot of memories over the last 50 years, with most of them pleasant. There were some detours along the way, but life is always a learning process. I think the only regret I have is the reason we were all brought together. I feel proud to have been a part of this process and sincerely hope your book is a help and inspiration to those who read it.

Love,
Dan

APPENDIX

It has been interesting to look back and recall the events of 48 years ago. There were no case-specific notations or logs to refer to in my research. When I visited Family and Children's Services of the Waterloo Region in May 2011, I was given a very warm welcome, and the agency affirmed my story as important history. I was given some of the minutes of the meetings of the CAS's board of directors, as well as the agency's annual reports for 1963 and 1964.

The minutes of the regular monthly meeting of the Board of Directors of the Children's Aid Society for the County of Waterloo dated November 21, 1963, make the first mention of our family's role in the foster care system:

Developments with respect to the opening of a small group care centre were outlined: Mr. and Mrs. "Evan" Thompson will be operating the home which will start with four boys. Mrs. Thompson is a university graduate, and has had child care experience with the Montreal Children's Services Centre and Metro Toronto Children's Aid Society. Mr. Thompson is the editor of the Waterloo Chronicle. Arrangements made included payment of $135 monthly for rent, the furnishing of the home with necessary equipment to remain the property of CAS and $60 per month for the care of each child.

The CAS's annual report for 1963 includes the following note from the president's report:

A major undertaking during the past year was the establishment of a small group care centre for boys. This was thought necessary because of the increasing number of children coming into our care whose background and history has been most disturbed. Foster parents selected for this undertaking must have more than average endurance, understanding and tolerance. Understandably, the costs of supporting children in such a home are somewhat higher than average. We are deeply indebted to the Board of Willow Hall (K-W Orphanage) for their generous assistance in furnishing the centre with necessary appliances.

The minutes of the regular monthly meeting of the Board of Directors of the Children's Aid Society for the County of Waterloo, dated September 17, 1964, give some indication of the perceived value of the pilot program:

At present, there are four homes where a subsidy is paid. The first special group home was established in November 1963 under the supervision of Mr. and Mrs. Thompson. At present there are two boys in their care. Under a similar arrangement, — is caring for two teenage girls in St. Jacobs. It is hoped these foster parents will care for these young people until no further care is needed for them ... these homes are well worth the investment we are making in them, although the foster parents are receiving special rates.

The minutes of the regular monthly meeting of the Board of Directors of the Children's Aid Society for the County of Waterloo, dated October 15, 1964, advocate for small-group foster care as a preventive measure:

... the establishment of two small group care centres for emotionally disturbed adolescents was the most progressive step taken by the board in recent years. Some foster homes have not been successful because the foster parents did not receive enough financial or moral support from the community or the agency ... the percentage of those who have serious emotional problems is steadily increasing ... our own foster home situation is comparatively good when compared with some others in the province. Dr. Ernst suggested that it might be well to explore very thoroughly what other agencies are doing to find out the causes of children getting into difficulty. If we continue to treat just the end results we are going to have a tremendous increase of children in care. It was suggested that with two universities in the City, this might be a good subject to study for students wishing to do their PhD theses.

I thought this was an excellent suggestion, but in the 1960s there was little understanding of our effort to address the cause of these children's problems.

The minutes of the regular monthly meeting of the Board of Directors of the Children's Aid Society of the County of Waterloo, dated November 19, 1964, include the following summaries of two meetings of the agency's Child Care Committee:

On October 29, the committee met to discuss the current trends in child care and plans were made to proceed in principle with exploring the establishment of a third group home. On November 5, members of the Child Care Committee met with the Services Committee of the Guelph Children's Aid Society along with the judges of the Juvenile and Family Court. The group met to discuss the need for an Observation Centre for short-term assessment of some children appearing in Juvenile and Family Court. The centre would not be a "detention home" but rather a professionally directed observation and evaluation centre. It could either be a house with foster parents providing a family setting, or a building designed specifically for this purpose. Accommodation for about 12 children would probably be adequate. Such a centre would not replace any existing facilities of the Society or any other agency in the area.

The committee proposed that a group home should be established to serve the immediate and urgent needs for the desirable minimum of six boys and a maximum of nine. It was moved that we give whatever authority is necessary to the Child Care Committee to proceed and implement this programme.

While CAS was creating group homes, there was little attention to documenting the needs and behaviours of the children involved.

At this point, our one-year term was coming to an end, and aside from the agency asking us to continue with Johnny, which we could not do, there were no further discussions or recommendations. But clearly there had been a positive reaction to our group home because a second was created for girls and a third was quickly found to replace ours.

The minutes of the regular monthly meeting of the Board of Directors of the Children's Aid Society for the County of Waterloo, dated December 17, 1964, outlines plans for continuing the program:

... the Committee met on November 24 to discuss the conditions of a contract planned for between our Society and the new parents who will be operating the Group Home for boys. The basic arrangements for the group care house parents in the Toronto Metro Society were used as a basis for study. The following recommendations were made:

A contract be drawn up between the Children's Aid Society and the parents who will be operating the home. If either party wishes to terminate the contract at any time, three months notice must be given. The parents should provide a home large enough for the accommodation of six boys in comfort, as well as taking care of their own family needs.

Additional terms provide for the payment to foster parents of $400 per month retainer plus $2.00 per day per child in care. The provision of equipment, beds, blankets, etc. for boys on behalf of the Children's Aid Society—which remains the property of the Children's Aid Society. They shall be responsible for arranging for their own domestic help, their time off and their vacation period at their own expense. The Society may require two telephones to accommodate the needs of boys and family.

The Group Home for girls … is to be given further study by the Finance Committee in light of the new home being established for boys.

The plans for a girls' home are detailed in the minutes of the regular meeting of the Board of Directors of the Children's Aid Society for the County of Waterloo, dated January 21, 1965:

A meeting of the Finance Committee was held on January 11 to discuss Group Home arrangements. It was the unanimous feeling of the Committee that similar arrangements be made with girls group home in the contract with the new boys home. The basic arrangement allows for $200 allowance for labour to the group home mother and $200 allowance toward rent, relief help, etc. to the father, plus $2.00 per day per child. The arrangement should be on the basis that six children would be cared for by either party.

Finally, there is this remark in the 1964 Children's Aid Society for the County of Waterloo Annual Report from the President:

Our society reported last year the establishment of a small group care centre for boys and acknowledged the assistance of the Board of Willow Hall (K-W Orphanage) in helping to furnish that centre. We have extended this policy during the past year with the establishment of a second group care centre to provide additional care for the more disturbed children that come into care.

BIBLIOGRAPHY

The Board of Directors of the Children's Aid Society for the County of Waterloo. Regular meeting minutes, 1963–65. Waterloo, ON.

Bowlby, John. "Forty-Four Juvenile Thieves: Their Characters and Home Lives." *International Journal of Psycho-Analysis* 25 (1944): 19–52.

————. "The Influence of Early Environment in the Development of Neurosis and Neurotic Character." *International Journal of Psycho-Analysis* 21 (1940): 1–25.

————. *Maternal Care and Mental Health.* World Health Organization, 1951.

Bratherton, Inge. "The Origins of Attachment Theory: John Bowlby and Mary Ainsworth." *Developmental Psychology* 28 (1992): 759–75.

The Children's Aid Society for the County of Waterloo. Annual reports, 1963–64. Waterloo, ON.

Acknowledgements

This is a story written from my heart so there was not a lot of research to be done. It did not occur to me as I wrote it in long hand that I would have to turn to my computer for the official work and communication. In doing so, I was supported by a large number of friends and colleagues who worked with me to bring the story to completion in this book.

A special thank you to Sigrid Macdonald, my first contact with an editor, who helped me sort out the tangle of stories in my mind. Her interest and encouragement made the realization of writing this story possible.

I have to thank Cassandra Kelly who researched current step-family trends. Realizing that it had been 25 years since I co-authored *Stepmothers: Exploring the Myth* with Kati Morrison, I saw that times had indeed changed, and that I should move to another segment of family life. So, I sidestepped to an earlier period of my life and in conjunction with some of my boys, decided to tell the important story about our pilot project with the group home.

This all came about because of Diane Thomas, who was interested in my stepmother work, but who also encouraged me to write about a myriad of interesting experiences that life has given me. Following Diane's untimely and dramatic death, I was unable to pick up my pen for a very long time. Thankfully, that grief has calmed, and I have been able to move forward with much gratitude to her.

The research that I did was to locate the orphanage that closed in 1962. They had donated monies to the Children's Aid Society which, in turn, used the funds to establish a group home for adolescent boys. My thanks to Barbara Ward at Kids Link in St. Agatha, Ontario who took time to show me around the facility, and gave me the opportunity to read some of the history when it was originally an orphanage. However, it was the wrong one. She later told me about an orphanage in Kitchener-Waterloo that turned out to be the source I was searching for.

My return to the Kitchener-Waterloo CAS now known as Family and Children's Services of the Waterloo Region was a great help to me. Welcomed by Allison Scott, the Executive Director, and some of her senior staff, I was thrilled with their interest in my project. They also inquired about their present day approaches to foster care. It was very helpful to be given relevant minutes of the Board of Directors as well as the Annual Reports for 1963 and 1964. Special thanks to Lovina Duguid who took time to search the archives for this information.

And because I only type with three fingers and continue to get into a stew when I have to deal with an attachment, I do sincerely thank

Joan Williams, Lise Dissant, Anne Alper, Joan Gilmore, Brenda Bates, Donna Mailloux, Judy Amey, Graham Amey, Sharon Ingram, Paul Richard, Nadya Burton, Ferial McAuliff, Audrey MacDonald, and Ann Flynn, and I am sure that there are others who stood by me and did much of the technical work.

My great appreciation goes to my colleagues who agreed to review and comment on my work: Mike Balla, Bob Glossop, Ron Ensom, Denis Kimberley, Dan Wiseman, and Kati Morrison. And, of course, Marion Balla for the forward.

Not to be forgotten is IUniverse and their wonderful staff for guiding me through the process of self-publishing.

I am grateful to all of you who helped me tell this story.